The BEZALEEL *Fellowship*

Equipping Laymen
to Serve the LORD in Local Churches

Dr. Tom Sexton

THE BEZALEEL FELLOWSHIP

FOREWORD

Pastor Tom Sexton's book on the Bible character of Bezaleel is truly excellent. He takes the compelling narrative of this man's life that is found in the Word of God and gives us the Christ honoring principles by which we must fashion and live our lives.

As I read this book, again and again I found myself saying: how did I not see what the Bible says about this man before? Every Christian should know what God says about Bezaleel!

Pastor Tom Sexton's book has wonderfully brought Bezaleel's life to our attention. This book is not just a good read; it is a life-changing read! I recommend it highly.

Dr. David Gibbs, Jr.
Founder and President
Christian Law Association

DEDICATION

This book is dedicated to Brother Rick Dugan
and all the faithful laymen who stand with their pastor
in the work of the LORD.

TABLE OF CONTENTS

Part I: Will Bezaleel Join the Critical Crowd (p. 51)
Part II: Will Bezaleel Compromise His Convictions (p. 55)
Part III: Will Bezaleel Use His Gift and Ability to Make the Golden Calf (p. 59)

INTRODUCTION

Bezaleel was a young man with whom most Bible believers are unfamiliar. He is one of the lost treasures. He was not a pastor, prophet, missionary, or gospel singer; he was a craftsman. He left behind a powerful testimony of how the LORD can use laymen.

God told Moses that He had given him Bezaleel to *"…make all that I have commanded thee…" **(Exodus 31:6b)**.* The purpose of Bezaleel's life was to help God's man. He influenced many men and women in his day and helped them find their place in the LORD's work. He taught people how to help God's man accomplish what the LORD had given him to do.

Those who help and encourage God's man will find themselves in a spiritual warfare with the forces of evil. The more valuable someone is to the LORD's work, the more intense the conflict.

Bezaleel built, with the help of all wise hearted people, the Tabernacle in the wilderness. God's final word about him is very powerful. ***Exodus 38:22**, "And Bezaleel the son of Uri, the son of Hur, of the tribe of Judah, made all that the LORD commanded Moses."*

May the LORD use these lessons to build men who can stand with God's man and accomplish God's will on this earth.

LESSON 1: MEET BEZALEEL

*"And the LORD spake unto Moses, saying, See, I have called by name
Bezaleel the son of Uri, the son of Hur, of the tribe of JUDAH"*
EXODUS 31:1-2

Studying the people that the LORD used to accomplish His plan and purpose down through the ages is one of my favorite methods of Bible study. The men and women of like passion, who had a heart for God and His work, left behind a message for all to follow. Every person that God puts on the pages of His Word has a message for us.

Bezaleel was one of those amazing men. He was not a preacher or prophet; he was a craftsman. He was, what we call today, a layman. God puts in people just like Bezaleel His gifts for mankind. He says in His Word, *"...in the hearts of all that are wise hearted I have put wisdom" (Exodus 31:6)*.

Bezaleel was given to Moses by God in *Exodus 31:6 "to make all that I have commanded thee."* Without Bezaleel, the work of the LORD would have been hindered, and Moses would not have accomplished all that he did for the LORD. What has the LORD put in us for His work?

As we study this remarkable young man, we will discover what all laymen need in order to help God's man do what He has called him to do. All men should find their place of service in the ministry of a local church.

May the LORD give us some Bezaleels - those who will use what the LORD has put in them to advance the cause of Christ. God is still looking for men to stand in the gap and to help their pastor do what God has put in his heart to accomplish.

There are several questions one must ask if he wants to learn about a person. As we study the life of Bezaleel, we must ask...

1. Who Was He?

Bezaleel was a slave in Egypt. There, he learned from the master craftsmen in Egypt how to be a craftsman. He is the only Bezaleel mentioned in the Bible; he was one of a kind. We are all one of a kind.

2. When Did He Live?

Bezaleel lived when Egypt was at its zenith. Egypt was what we call today a world superpower. He lived when God's people were in bondage. He lived when God sent Moses to Pharaoh. Egypt was nothing compared to God who is *"...all power."*

3. Did He Face Any Challenges Or Difficulties In Life?

Bezaleel was a slave, and the Egyptian taskmasters were very cruel. He also witnessed the collapse of a world power, Egypt. He saw firsthand what happens to a nation that forgets God.

4. Who Influenced His Life?

Bezaleel was influenced by the craftsmen in Egypt, and he was influenced by Moses. Without Moses, Bezaleel would have lived and died, and no one would know his name. Moses made it possible for Bezaleel to use all that he had learned in Egypt for the Lord's work.

When leaders get direction from the LORD, they make it possible for others to serve and use their gifts for the LORD and His work.

5. What Impact Did He Make On Life?

Bezaleel built the Tabernacle in the wilderness. He personally trained many men and women in the work of the LORD. Bezaleel's life made it possible for the LORD to continue His plan for the ages.

The testimony of Bezaleel that God gives says it all:

> *"And Bezaleel the son of Uri, the son of Hur, of the tribe of Judah, made all that the LORD commanded Moses."* Exodus 38:22

What will be our epitaph? If we follow God's plan for the ages, others will be able to follow behind us and continue God's great work.

LESSONS

1. God knows what is going on in our lives.

Exodus 3:7, *"And the LORD said, I have surely seen the affliction of My people which are in Egypt, and have heard their cry by reason of their taskmasters; for I know their sorrows"*

The LORD truly does know our heartache. He sees and hears our sorrows. We may not see Him, but He always sees us. His eyes are always upon us.

2. There are always two kingdoms that want you.

Both kingdoms need labourers. The LORD says in ***Exodus 31:2,*** *"See, I have called by name Bezaleel…"* and in ***Luke 22:31,*** *"…Satan hath desired to have you…"* The LORD wants to use us, and the devil wants to use us.

Which kingdom will we build? Remember, the kingdoms of this world will all pass away, *"…but he that doeth the will of God abideth for ever"* ***(I John 2:15-17, v. 17).***

3. Every life influences others – good or bad.

Exodus 31:6, *"And I, behold, I have given with him Aholiab, the son of Ahisamach, of the tribe of Dan: and in the hearts of all that are wise hearted I have put wisdom, that they may make all that I have commanded thee"*

Exodus 35:34, *"And He hath put in his heart that he may teach, both he, and Aholiab, the son of Ahisamach, of the tribe of Dan."*

These two men, Bezaleel and Aholiab, were going to teach others. They lived in such a way that they could influence others for the LORD. What a blessing it is to sit at the feet of men who love the LORD and His work!

God's Word says in ***Romans 14:7,*** *"For none of us liveth to himself, and no man dieth to himself."* We each have influence. We should ask ourselves, "Whose life am I influencing?" We need to build our influence, recognize that we can break our influence, and ask the Lord to broaden our influence.

4. Men have a brief period to live.

Exodus 31:2a, *"See, I have called by name Bezaleel…"*

Bezaleel comes and goes. We never hear of him again.

James 4:14 reminds us, *"Whereas ye know not what shall be on the morrow. For what is your life? It is even a vapour, that appeareth for a little time, and then vanisheth away."* Life is very brief. What we do for the LORD, we must do quickly. It is not **how long** we live, it is **how** we live that counts.

There are two great decisions all men should make in life.

- **Make sure that you know Christ as your personal Saviour.**

  I John 5:13, *"These things have I written unto you that believe on the name of the Son of God; that ye may know that ye have eternal life, and that ye may believe on the name of the Son of God."*

  If you do not know Christ as your personal Saviour, please turn to the last pages of this book and read how to know Him today.

- **Give your life to do His will.**

  Ephesians 5:17, *"Wherefore be ye not unwise, but understanding what the will of the Lord is."*

  I am asking the LORD to reveal to men and women what He wants done in this world and that those who are wise hearted will give their lives to do God's will.

LESSON 2: THE CALLING OF BEZALEEL

"See, I have called by name Bezaleel the son of Uri, the son of Hur, of the tribe of Judah..." **EXODUS 31:2**

In this lesson we are going to answer three of the most important questions on the minds and hearts of all men:

- *Who am I?*
- *Where did I come from?*
- *Why am I here?*

Answering these three questions gives meaning to life. It has been said that when you are born, you cry and others rejoice, but if you have lived a life of purpose, when you die others cry and you rejoice.

Bezaleel's life made others to rejoice. He could have said, "I know who I am, I know where I came from, and I know why I am here."

Every life has a great purpose. Bezaleel did the will of God with his life, and in his life we can see how the LORD prepares all men for His plan and purpose.

1. Who Am I?

Notice in ***Exodus 31:2***, *"...I have called by name Bezaleel...."* This is the only Bezaleel in the Bible. His name means, "God is protection." Bezaleel was one of a kind; he was very unique.

Maybe we can understand this question of *who we are* by asking *what we are*. What are we?

- ## We are God's creation.

  Genesis 1:26-27, v. 27, *"...So God created man in His own image, in the image of God created He him; male and female created He them."*

  God made us in His image. That means that we were made to live forever. We are eternal beings, and we will spend eternity somewhere.

- ## We are all very unique.

  Psalm 139:14, *"I will praise Thee; for I am fearfully and wonderfully made: marvellous are Thy works; and that my soul knoweth right well."*

  There are no two people just alike. Even identical twins are not identical. God could have made us all the same, but He made us all different. It's okay to be you. God wants you to be you. Do not go through life copying someone else - be who you are and what you are.

  The little boy said to his mother that he learned in Sunday School that God made him, and "God don't make junk."

  Who are you? If you are not you, then who will be you?

2. Where Did I Come From?

Continue reading in ***Exodus 31:2*** and notice, *"...the son of Uri, the son of Hur, of the tribe of Judah."*

Bezaleel had a family, and he had a family history. The truth of the matter is that none of us just showed up. We all got here through a family. Our Christian family connects us to a godly line of people.

- **His father and grandfather were faithful men.**

Bezaleel was *"the son of Uri, the son of Hur."* He came from a family of faithful men. His father was Uri - his name means "fire." His grandfather was Hur - he was one of the men who held up the hands of Moses during the battle against Amalek.

Even if we did not come from a family of faithful men, we all have the power to **start** a godly line. The children of Israel told the LORD that their fathers had eaten sour grapes, and their life was affected by it *(Ezekiel 18:2)*. The LORD taught them that every life was responsible and accountable to Him and that we cannot blame our failures on our fathers.

3. Why Am I Here?

Notice again in *Exodus 31:2, "...I have called...."*

God said that *He* called Bezaleel. The LORD had a purpose for his life. Someone once said, "The greatest knowledge in all the world is to know the will of God, and life's greatest success is to do it."

- **God has called us.**

God is looking for laymen. The Bible says, *"For ye see your calling, brethren, how that not many wise men after the flesh, not many mighty, not many noble, are called" (I Corinthians 1:26).*

The LORD calls men to His work. Some men are called early in life, and some men are called later in life. We will see His calling for our life as we obey His command with our life. As we obey and serve Him, we see where we fit. Every man can fit in God's work.

- ## God has chosen us.

I Corinthians 1:27-29, *"But God hath chosen the foolish things of the world to confound the wise; and God hath chosen the weak things of the world to confound the things which are mighty; And base things of the world, and things which are despised, hath God chosen, yea, and things which are not, to bring to nought things that are: That no flesh should glory in His presence."*

What does it mean to be chosen?

John 15:16, *"Ye have not chosen Me, but I have chosen you, and ordained you, that ye should go and bring forth fruit, and that your fruit should remain: that whatsoever ye shall ask of the Father in My name, He may give it you."*

Look carefully at this verse, *"...He may give it you."* It does not say "He may give it *to* you." It says that God wants to give us *to* something. The question we each must ask ourselves is this:

Am I willing to let the LORD give me to something?

If the answer is yes, then we will be able to answer these three powerful questions.

LESSONS

1. There is only one of us and Christ died for our sins.

Ephesians 4:24, *"And that ye put on the new man, which after God is created in righteousness and true holiness."*

We become the *"...new man..."* by knowing Christ as our personal Saviour *(John 1:11-13; II Corinthians 5:17).*

2. There is a great purpose for our existence.

Ephesians 2:10, *"For we are his workmanship, created in Christ Jesus unto good works, which God hath before ordained that we should walk in them."*

The LORD has a *"...work..."* for every man. One day we will give an account to God for that work ***(II Corinthians 5:10; I Corinthians 3:13-15)***.

3. The only way to find our life's purpose is to surrender.

Romans 12:1-2, *"I beseech you therefore, brethren, by the mercies of God, that ye present your bodies a living sacrifice, holy, acceptable unto God, which is your reasonable service. And be not conformed to this world: but be ye transformed by the renewing of your mind, that ye may prove what is that good, and acceptable, and perfect, will of God."*

The Word of God says that His will is *"...good...acceptable...and perfect...."* We are here to do His will. The only way to find God's will for your life is to give your life for His will. The will of God for our life is to help everyone else do the will of God with their life.

What is God's will for all? He is *"not willing that any should perish, but that all should come to repentance" **(II Peter 3:9).*** He wants all men to be saved. What would happen if we who know Christ as our personal Saviour gave our lives to do His will?

Lesson 3: Bezaleel,
Filled with the Spirit of God

"And I have filled him with the spirit of God..."
Exodus 31:1-5, v. 3a

The Bible says in **Ephesians 5:18**, *"And be not drunk with wine, wherein is excess; but be filled with the Spirit."* Is there a difference in a man who is filled with the Spirit of God and a man who is not filled with the Spirit of God? Is there a difference in a man who is drunk with wine and a man who is not drunk with wine?

The answer to both questions is, "Yes!" There is a difference in a person who is filled and a person who is not filled with the Spirit of God. It is a noticeable difference.

I once asked Dr. Lee Roberson (my beloved pastor) how one could tell if a person was filled with the Spirit of God. His answer was heart searching. He said, "It is easy to tell when a man is <u>not</u> filled with the Holy Spirit; he is restless, discontent, and has no spiritual fruit in his life." Upon that answer, I had to find a place alone and ask God to fill me.

The subject of being filled with the Holy Spirit cannot be fully covered in one lesson or one thousand lessons. My purpose in this lesson is to show some simple truths that all laymen need. Remember, Bezaleel was not a preacher; he was a layman who did a powerful work for God.

The questions I would like to consider in this lesson are:

- *What is the filling of the Spirit?*

- *Why is it so important in the life of all believers?*

- *How can someone be filled with the Spirit of God?*

1. What Is The Filling Of The Holy Spirit?

Ephesians 5:18, *"And be not drunk with wine, wherein is excess; but be filled with the Spirit."*

The answer to this question has been under discussion for hundreds of years. I have heard this subject discussed by Bible teachers who were as dry as a desert and by zealous new believers who could not quote two verses on the subject.

D. L. Moody tried to explain it to some pastors in his day, and R. A. Torrey in his book, *Why God Used D. L. Moody,* said Moody was very saddened by their response.

Curtis Hutson, my dear friend who is with the LORD, tried to illustrate it by using his wife, Jerrie, as an example and nearly died prematurely. He said, "Being filled with the Spirit is having more of God. For example, when I got married I got all of Jerrie, my wife, but now I have more of her." Everyone but Jerrie laughed.

Dr. Roberson said, "It is the difference in men. Men and women who are used of God are filled with the Holy Spirit, and people who are not mightily used of the Lord are not filled with the Spirit of God."

- **We know that we are born into the family of God by the Spirit.**

  John 1:11-13, v. 13; *"Which were born, not of blood, nor of the will of the flesh, nor of the will of man, but of God."*

  Ephesians 2:1, *"And you hath He quickened, who were dead in trespasses and sins."*

  John 3:5-6, *"Jesus answered, Verily, verily, I say unto thee, Except a man be born of water and of the Spirit, he cannot enter into the kingdom of God. That which is born of the flesh is flesh; and that which is born of the Spirit is spirit."*

- ## We know that we are sealed by the Spirit.

  Ephesians 4:30, *"And grieve not the holy Spirit of God, whereby ye are sealed unto the day of redemption."*

  Have you experienced that spiritual birth?

- ## What does it mean to be filled with the Spirit?

  Let me say this for now. To be filled with the Spirit means to be empty of self and filled with God. Every area of our life is changed.

  Mark 12:30, *"And thou shalt love the Lord thy God with **all** thy heart, and with **all** thy soul, and with **all** thy mind, and with **all** thy strength: this is the first commandment."*

  Let God control *"...all..."* of your life.
  - *"all thy heart"* = what you love
  - *"all thy soul"* = every room of your life
  - *"all thy mind"* = what you think about
  - *"all thy strength"* = the power you live by

2. Why Is It So Important?

Exodus 31:3a, *"And I have filled him with the spirit of God..."*

This is the first thing given to us about Bezaleel. This is where God begins. He first fills Bezaleel with the Spirit, then the rest follows.

*"But seek ye **first** the kingdom of God, and His righteousness; and all these things shall be added unto you."* ***Matthew 6:33***

The Holy Spirit knows what we need in order to do what God has given us to do. God knows how to build men because He knows what is next.

I Corinthians 2:12, *"Now we have received, not the spirit of the world, but the spirit which is of God; that we **might know** the things that are freely given to us of God."*

The Christian life is a building process. We are to add to our faith *(II Peter 1:5-9).* You cannot have what is next if you do not get what is first.

What is next for you? Do you believe that the LORD knows what you need next? We do not know what lies ahead in our future, but the LORD knows. He will put in us all we need to succeed in His will and work. He wants all believers to finish right *(Ecclesiastes 7:8)*.

3. How Can I Be Filled With The Spirit Of God?

Ephesians 5:18, *"...Be filled with the Spirit."*

- **Empty yourself.**

  I Corinthians 15:31, *"...I die daily."*

  You have Christ *(Ephesians 3:17)*, but does He have you? And does He have *all* of you?

- **Ask God to cleanse you.**

  I John 1:9, *"If we confess our sins, He is faithful and just to forgive us our sins, and to cleanse us from all unrighteousness."*

  God will not fill a dirty vessel. People do not want water from a dirty cup.

- **Ask God to fill and use you.**

  Luke 11:13, *"If ye then, being evil, know how to give good gifts unto your children: how much more shall your heavenly Father give the Holy Spirit to them that ask Him?"*

  The people who make a difference are those who are filled with the Spirit of God. Give God control of your life *(Galatians 5:16-17)*.

People who are filled are in one accord.

Acts 4:31, *"And when they had prayed, the place was shaken where they were assembled together; and they were all filled with the Holy Ghost, and they spake the word of God with boldness."*

God puts us together because we need each other to complete the work that He has given us to do. The only way that we can work together and be in one accord is to be filled with the Holy Spirit.

Are you filled with the Holy Spirit?

LESSON 4: BEZALEEL, FILLED WITH WISDOM

"...I have filled him with...wisdom..." EXODUS 31:1-6, v. 3

"...And in the hearts of all that are wise hearted I have put wisdom, that they may make all that I have commanded thee" EXODUS 31:1-6, v. 6b

The LORD gives us a list of all that He put in Bezaleel. At the top of the list is *"the Spirit of God...."* This is the starting place for all who desire to be used of God. The next on the list is *"...wisdom...."* In this lesson, we will ask the LORD to give us wisdom in order to understand how He builds men.

What is wisdom? Where does wisdom come from? Do we need wisdom today?

I know of no subject that is more important to the child of God than this subject of wisdom. Today we see such a lack of wisdom in decision-making among Christians, and it is reflected in their lives.

1. Wisdom Prepares Us to Meet God

"The fear of the LORD is the beginning of wisdom..." **Proverbs 9:10a**

To fear the LORD does not mean to walk around thinking that God is going to kill us or do some horrible thing to us. To fear the LORD means that we are sober to the fact that one day we will give an account of our life to Him.

All believers will one day appear before the Judgment Seat of Christ.

II Corinthians 5:10, *"For we must all appear before the judgment seat of Christ; that every one may receive the things done in his body, according to that he hath done, whether it be good or bad."*

The LORD Jesus spoke much about *"...that day...."* Paul spoke much about *"...that day..."* when Christ shall come. He lived for *"...that day...."* Understanding the seriousness of that day gives wisdom. I want to have a good day that day, and I am for anyone who wants to help me have a good day at the Judgment Seat of Christ.

What people think about *that* day will have an impact on how they live *this* day. Every day that we live should better prepare us for *"...that day."*

2. Wisdom Helps Us Put The Things Of Life In Proper Order

Proverbs 8:11, *"For wisdom is better than rubies; and all the things that may be desired are not to be compared to it."*

All the wealth that would be needed to build the Tabernacle would pass through the hands of Bezaleel. What would Moses have taught Bezaleel about *"...the treasures of Egypt..." (Hebrews 11:23-26)*? Before Bezaleel was given the treasures from Egypt, he was given wisdom from God.

It takes wisdom to live in accordance with the *"love nots"* of *I John 2:15-17*. A man with wisdom will not be turned by the riches of this world. We have the power, while we are alive, to exchange that of which we have been made stewards in this life for treasures in Heaven *(Matthew 6:19-20)*.

3. Wisdom Makes It Possible To Work With People

Exodus 31:6b, *"...And in the hearts of all that are wise hearted I have put wisdom, that they may make all that I have commanded thee"*

There is no such thing as "people skills" in the Bible. It is called wisdom. We need wisdom to work with the many different people in our churches.

Wisdom prepares us to meet God, keeps us from being captured by riches, and makes it possible for us to work with people. Are you a wise man? God's Word says in *James 1:5,* *"If any of you lack wisdom, let him ask of God, that giveth to all men liberally, and upbraideth not; and it shall be given him."*

- **A wise man knows Christ as their personal Saviour.**

  I Corinthians 1:23-24, *"But we preach Christ crucified, unto the Jews a stumblingblock, and unto the Greeks foolishness; But unto them which are called, both Jews and Greeks, Christ the power of God, and the wisdom of God."*

  Do you know Christ as *your* personal Savior?

- **A wise man is in touch with the Spirit of wisdom.**

  Acts 6:3, *"Wherefore, brethren, look ye out among you seven men of honest report, full of the Holy Ghost and wisdom, whom we may appoint over this business."*

  Acts 6:10, *"And they were not able to resist the wisdom and the spirit by which he spake."*

  Get wisdom from the One who indwells you.

  I John 2:27, *"But the anointing which ye have received of Him abideth in you, and ye need not that any man teach you: but as the same anointing teacheth you of all things, and is truth, and is no lie, and even as it hath taught you, ye shall abide in Him."*

- **A wise man is one who knows the Scriptures.**

  II Timothy 3:15, *"And that from a child thou hast known the holy scriptures, which are able to make thee wise unto salvation through faith which is in Christ Jesus."*

  Knowing the Scriptures delivers from destruction.

  Psalm 107:20, *"He sent His word, and healed them, and delivered them from their destructions."*

  Hosea 4:6a, *"My people are destroyed for lack of knowledge..."*

- **A wise man wins others to Christ.**

  Proverbs 11:30, *"The fruit of the righteous is a tree of life; and he that winneth souls is wise."*

  Daniel 12:3, *"And they that be wise shall shine as the brightness of the firmament; and they that turn many to righteousness as the stars for ever and ever."*

  We will all reflect the kind of life we lived.

LESSON 5: BEZALEEL,
A MAN WITH UNDERSTANDING

"And I have filled him with the spirit of God, in wisdom, and in understanding, and in knowledge, and in all manner of workmanship"
EXODUS 31:3

Bezaleel is the first person in the Bible that God said had understanding. This does not mean he was the first person who had understanding; he is just the first person mentioned in the Bible that God said had understanding.

Understanding makes it possible to work together. The more a person understands, the more valuable they are. This is true in the world, and it is certainly true in the LORD's work.

Understanding means to see how everything fits together, to be able to see the big picture. People with understanding can see the finished product and know how to use different people to get there.

Moses could not have accomplished all that he did in life without enlisting the help of all the people who came out of Egypt. He needed someone who could work with the many different types of people who each had various skills and backgrounds. Bezaleel was that someone.

Bezaleel was the man who put everyone to work. He found a job for all to do. The men and women who followed his leadership helped Moses to accomplish what God had put in his heart to do.

Every **church** and **ministry** needs men with understanding in order for people to work together and to be in a spirit of one accord. Understanding makes it possible to know **what** people can do in the LORD's work.

1. Only The LORD Can Open Our Mind Of Understanding

Luke 24:45, *"Then opened He their understanding, that they might understand the scriptures"*

The road to Emmaus leads away from the place God wants you.

The reason these two men were on this road is because they did not understand what the LORD was doing.

Without understanding, we will be on the wrong path.

2. The Measure Of Our Understanding Is The Measure Of Our Maturity

I Corinthians 13:11, *"When I was a child, I spake as a child, I understood as a child, I thought as a child: but when I became a man, I put away childish things."*

Children have a hard time understanding. They cannot see the big picture of life. They live in a small world with a small mind of understanding.

The same can be said of a child of God who has not matured in the LORD.

Exodus 32:29, *"...Consecrate yourselves to day to the LORD, even every man upon his son, and upon his brother; that he may bestow upon you a blessing this day."*

The LORD said that He wanted to bless Israel, but did Israel understand? Do *we* understand how much He wants to bless us?

3. Pray For Understanding

In Paul's prayer for the people of the church in Ephesus, he asked the LORD to open their minds of understanding:

*"...The eyes of your understanding being enlightened; that ye may know what is the hope of His calling, and what the riches of the glory of His inheritance in the saints..." **Ephesians 1:15-18, v. 18***

They had been given a great opportunity and the door was open to them, but **they** had to see the big picture.

In our text, Moses has led the children of Israel out of Egypt, and now the next chapter in God's plan for the ages is about to unfold. Moses needs someone to help him who understands what God is doing. Bezaleel (a layman) is that man.

We know that the LORD has more to be accomplished on this earth. If this were not true, the rapture would have taken place. It is the responsibility of all who pastor to discover what God has in His heart to be done. God will always give men like Bezaleel to a pastor who is given to the will of God.

4. What All Believers Need to Understand About the LORD's Work

- **The work of the LORD is for all believers.**

"Go ye..." (Matthew 28:19-20). All believers are commanded to go. Bob Hughes, the great missionary to Asia, said, "Who needs a call when they have a command."

The greatest need in the LORD's work is, and always has been, labourers. *"...The harvest truly is plenteous, but the labourers are few" (Matthew 9:37)*.

This does not mean that the LORD wants men to quit their jobs and join the church staff, but it does mean that the LORD Jesus wants all men to find their place of service in their local church.

- **The work of the LORD is to be carried out through the ministries of local churches around the world.**

"...Go ye into all the world, and preach the gospel to every creature" (Mark 16:15).

The church has a mission from God. The church has been commissioned to take the Gospel to every person.

Keeping the main thing the main thing is the responsibility of the pastor who *"...must give account" (Hebrews 13:17).*

- **The work of the LORD is fourfold.**

"...Ye shall receive power, after that the Holy Ghost is come upon you: and ye shall be witnesses unto Me both in Jerusalem, and in all Judaea, and in Samaria, and unto the uttermost part of the earth" (Acts 1:8).

The little word *"...both..."* means "at the same time." The people who are responsible for the work in *"...Jerusalem..."* are the same people who are responsible for the other three areas. No area is to be left out. No person should be overlooked. *"...Go ye into all the world...."*

As we give our life to do God's will, we will find God's will for our life.

LESSON 6: BEZALEEL, FILLED WITH KNOWLEDGE

"And Moses said unto the children of Israel, See, the LORD hath called by name Bezaleel the son of Uri, the son of Hur, of the tribe of Judah; And He hath filled him with the spirit of God, in wisdom, in understanding, and in knowledge, and in all manner of workmanship" **Exodus 35:30-31**

As we continue our study in the life of Bezaleel, we see that he was filled *"...in knowledge...."*

Bezaleel was going to oversee the construction of the Tabernacle in the wilderness. He would be working with many different skilled men and women. He had to know what they needed to accomplish their part in God's plan.

He was filled with the Spirit of God. He had wisdom to work with the different types of people and had an understanding of how everything fits together, but he needed knowledge to know what everyone needed in order to do their part.

The LORD knew what was ahead for Bezaleel. If Bezaleel was going to succeed in life, he had to be complete. He must have knowledge.

How does someone get knowledge? There are no shortcuts to getting knowledge. You must work at it.

1. You Must Find Someone With Knowledge

Proverbs 15:7, *"The lips of the wise disperse knowledge: but the heart of the foolish doeth not so."*

All who are wise have found someone with wisdom (knowledge) to teach them.

"Wise men lay up knowledge..." ***(Proverbs 10:14)*** for the next generation.

Bezaleel's life had crossed the path of those who had knowledge. You can learn from the world without love for the world.

2. Remember the LORD is the Source of All Knowledge

I Samuel 2:3, *"...The LORD is a God of knowledge, and by him actions are weighed."*

3. You Must Be The Kind Of Person Others Want To Teach

Proverbs 14:18, *"The simple inherit folly: but the prudent are crowned with knowledge."*

Bezaleel would have been a pleasure to work with – a reasonable young man with personal discipline.

People want to teach men who have character; no one wants to teach a know-it-all. Be a reasonable man. Use good judgment when working with others.

4. You Must Master The Basics

Hebrews 5:12, *"For when for the time ye ought to be teachers, ye have need that one teach you again ..."*

You must have a good foundation in order to build a future. Men who do not master the basics do not become master builders.

What are the basics of the Christian life? We all know what the five-star rating means. It means excellence; the best. Five Star Christians are practicing Christians. Work at becoming a Five Star Christian.

The five stars that make up the Five Star Christian Life are the foundations of the Christian life. They produce the roots that allow believers to be planted in the faith. Each star produces certain fruit, and in order to have the fruit, we must have the root. Dr. Lee Roberson said, "Every victory in the believer's life is the result of doing these five things and every problem in the believer's life can be traced to the neglect of these five things."

What are the five stars that make up the Five Star Christian?

☆ The First Star Is Bible Reading

Acts 2:42, *"And they continued stedfastly in the apostles' <u>doctrine</u>..."*

Revelation 1:3, *"Blessed is he that readeth, and they that hear the words of this prophecy..."*

We need to know the importance of God's Word. We should read it, incorporate it into our daily life, and know its message.

Bible reading produces:
- **Faith (*Romans 10:17*)**
- **Direction for Life (*Psalm 119:105*)**
- **Deliverance from Personal Battles (*Psalm 107:20*)**

☆ The Second Star Is Prayer

Acts 2:42, *"And they continued…in* <u>*prayers*</u>*."*

I Thessalonians 5:17, *"Pray without ceasing."*

People need to know that their prayers make a difference. Learn to keep a prayer list and to talk about how the LORD has answered your prayers.

Prayer produces:
- **The Blessing of God on Our Lives** *(James 4:2)*
- **A Closeness to the LORD** *(James 4:8)*
- **Rewards in Heaven** *(Revelation 5:8)*

☆ The Third Star Is Faithfulness To Church

Acts 2:42, *"And they continued stedfastly in…*<u>*fellowship*</u>*…"*

Hebrews 10:25, *"Not forsaking the assembling of ourselves together, as the manner of some is; but exhorting one another: and so much the more, as ye see the day approaching."*

People need to know that church is not just a place to attend but is a place to serve the LORD.

Faithfulness to church will produce:
- **Encouragement in Their Life** *(Hebrews 10:25, 3:13)*
- **Fellowship with Like-Minded People** *(Acts 2:42, I John 1:7)*
- **The Joy of the LORD in Their Life** *(Psalm 122:1, Neh. 8:10)*

☆ The Fourth Star Is Giving

Acts 2:45, *"And sold their possessions and goods, and parted them to all men, as every man had need."*

Luke 6:38*, "Give, and it shall be given unto you; good measure, pressed down, and shaken together, and running over, shall men give into your bosom. For with the same measure that ye mete withal it shall be measured to you again."*

People need to be taught how to be good stewards of their time, talent, and treasure ***(I Corinthians 4:2)***.

Being a good steward produces:
- **The Windows of Heaven Open in Our Lives** *(Malachi 3:10)*
- **Being Blessed by Others** *(Luke 6:38)*
- **Treasures in Heaven** *(Matthew 6:20-21)*

☆ The Fifth Star Is Witnessing

Acts 2:46, *"And they, continuing daily with one accord in the temple, and breaking bread from house to house, did eat their meat with gladness and singleness of heart"*

Acts 1:8, *"But ye shall receive power, after that the Holy Ghost is come upon you: and ye shall be witnesses unto Me both in Jerusalem, and in all Judaea, and in Samaria, and unto the uttermost part of the earth."*

Being a faithful witness produces:
- **Rewards at the Judgment Seat of Christ** *(I Thess. 2:19-20)*
- **Compassion in a Believer's Life** *(Matthew 9:35-36)*
- **Eternal Joy Over a Life Given to the LORD**
  (Proverbs 11:30, Daniel 12:3)

LESSONS

1. Realize you need others to complete the work God has given us.

I Corinthians 12:12-21, v. 21, "...The eye cannot say unto the hand, I have no need of thee: nor again the head to the feet, I have no need of you."

There is no one that is good at everything. Know where people fit in God's work. Do not put a "square" person in a round hole or a "round" person in a square hole.

2. Accept people for who they are and what they are.

I Corinthians 12:22-25, v. 22, "Nay, much more those members of the body, which seem to be more feeble, are necessary"

People will do their best for those who see their worth. It is true that people do not care how much you know until they know how much you care.

A person who gets the credit for the job must reflect honour to others.

Romans 13:7, "Render therefore to all their dues: tribute to whom tribute is due; custom to whom custom; fear to whom fear; honour to whom honour."

3. Be a team player.

I Corinthians 3:9, *"For we are labourers together with God: ye are God's husbandry, ye are God's building."*

You can be on the team and not be a team player.

Some use others to make themselves look better, and some use their talent and gifts to make others better.

4. It is a privilege to work with God's man.

Exodus 31:6, *"... They may make all that I have commanded thee"*

When it is all said and done, only one person will give an account of the local church and all its ministries.

Hebrews 13:17, *"Obey them that have the rule over you, and submit yourselves: for they watch for your souls, as they that must give account, that they may do it with joy, and not with grief: for that is unprofitable for you."*

5. It is the LORD's name that must be remembered.

I Kings 8:60, *"That all the people of the earth may know that the LORD is God..."*

Do we want all the people of the earth to know God or to know us?

"He must increase, but I must decrease" *(John 3:30).*

LESSON 7: BEZALEEL, FILLED WITH ALL MANNER OF WORKMANSHIP

"And I have filled him with the spirit of God, in wisdom, and in understanding, and in knowledge, and in all manner of workmanship"
EXODUS 31:3

In this lesson, we will see the believer and his work. The word *work* is a four-letter word that most Christians do not like. When they hear the word, they have a negative reaction. Yes, we are saved by grace, but we are saved *"...unto good works..." (Ephesians 2:10).*

Bezaleel had the responsibility of helping everyone find their place of service. He had to find where people fit in the building of the Tabernacle.

There is a job for every believer. There should be no unemployment in the LORD's work. The "Golden Rule" in a church should be to accept people where they are, win them to Christ, and help them find something to do for our coming Saviour. The goal of every leader in the work of the LORD is to help people find their place in the great work the LORD has given them.

1. There Is A Work For Every Believer

I Corinthians 3:11-13, v. 13, "Every man's work shall be made manifest: for the day shall declare it, because it shall be revealed by fire; and the fire shall try every man's work of what sort it is."

If every man's work is going to be tried, then it stands to reason that every man has a work. Serious-minded believers live with *"...that day..."* in their heart and mind. The day we meet the LORD Jesus and give an account of our life and work is the most sobering thought a Christian can have. I am for anyone who wants me to have a good day that day.

John 6:29, *"Jesus answered and said unto them, This is the work of God, that ye believe on Him whom He hath sent."* The work of believers is to believe. We must *"...believe..."* that the LORD has something for us.

2. The Work Began With Our Life Will Continue Until The Trumpet Sounds

Philippians 1:6, *"Being confident of this very thing, that He which hath begun a good work in you will perform it until the day of Jesus Christ"*

- **Every work has a beginning.**

  Mark 5:20, *"And he departed, and began to publish in Decapolis how great things Jesus had done for him: and all men did marvel."*

  The man that Christ saved had a starting place. The Bible says, *"...and he...began...."*

  Every believer has the power to begin something for God. What we begin can become a mighty movement for God. Only the LORD knows how far our work will go.

  Remember that it takes the same thing to keep something going that it did to get it going.

- **Every work began for God will continue until the day of Christ.**

  Philippians 1:6, *"...until the day of Jesus Christ"*

  We may lose track with what is going on, but the LORD keeps good records. He has a book with all of our wanderings *(Psalm 56:8)*. He knows every life that has been touched by our life *(Philippians 2:16)*.

  Bezaleel did something with his life that influenced many generations to follow. Do not let your life pass without beginning something for God.

A Dedicated Worker's Pledge

1. I Will Live Above Reproach

I Thessalonians 5:22, *"Abstain from all appearance of evil."*

Every worker should be a practicing Christian. By that I mean that Christians should practice what they believe *every* day, not just on the LORD's day.

2. I Will Work At Staying In One Accord With Other Believers

Acts 2:1, *"And when the day of Pentecost was fully come, they were all with one accord in one place."*

Acts 2:46, *"And they, continuing daily with one accord in the temple, and breaking bread from house to house, did eat their meat with gladness and singleness of heart"*

One person can hurt the spirit of a church. Staying in fellowship and one accord creates a powerful spirit in a church. This is the secret to having God's blessings. Every time we read of one accord in the Bible, there is a great moving of God in the church.

3. I Will Stand With Leadership

II Timothy 4:17, *"...The LORD stood with me..."*

People sometimes say, "I'm behind you, preacher." I often remind them of what Jesus said to Peter, *"...Get thee behind Me, Satan...."* Don't stand behind; stand beside. If you stand beside, you will both get shot. Stand *with* leadership.

4. I Will Work At Keeping "The Sunny Side Up"

I Thessalonians 5:18, *"In every thing give thanks: for this is the will of God in Christ Jesus concerning you."*

The little word *"...in..."* is the key to understanding this verse. We would change that word to "after." It is hard to give thanks *in* trouble or heartache. Anyone can look back and give thanks, but it takes a mature Christian to give thanks *in* problems and disappointments.

Be a believer that lifts the spirits of others. Remember the joy of the LORD is still our strength *(Nehemiah 8:10).*

5. I Will Be Faithful

I Corinthians 4:2, *"Moreover it is required in stewards, that a man be found faithful."*

Be a "Three to Thrive" believer. Be in the house of the Lord Sunday morning, Sunday evening, and for the midweek service. You may not be the best singer or teacher or anything else, but you can be faithful. Determine to be faithful.

LESSON 8: BEZALEEL AND THE ADVERSARY

*"And when the people saw that Moses delayed to come down out of the mount, the people gathered themselves together unto Aaron, and said unto him, Up, make us gods, which shall go before us; for as for this Moses, the man that brought us up out of the land of Egypt, we wot not what is become of him. And Aaron said unto them, Break off the golden earrings, which are in the ears of your wives, of your sons, and of your daughters, and bring them unto me. And all the people brake off the golden earrings which were in their ears, and brought them unto Aaron. And he received them at their hand, and fashioned it with a graving tool, after he had made it a molten calf: and they said, These be thy gods, O Israel, which brought thee up out of the land of Egypt. And when Aaron saw it, he built an altar before it; and Aaron made proclamation, and said, To morrow is a feast to the LORD. And they rose up early on the morrow, and offered burnt offerings, and brought peace offerings; and the people sat down to eat and to drink, and rose up to play." **EXODUS 32:1-6***

*"Be sober, be vigilant; because your adversary the devil, as a roaring lion, walketh about, seeking whom he may devour" **I PETER 5:8***

Bezaleel was a man who had been prepared by the LORD to help Moses accomplish the great work God had given him to do. Moses was to build the Tabernacle in the wilderness, and he needed Bezaleel. God had Bezaleel ready, but Satan had a way and plan to stop him. Bezaleel had to move past this trap before he would be able to do what God had called him to do. What the devil used on Bezaleel is the same thing he uses on God's people today.

In this three-part lesson we will see how the devil works to destroy the influence and character of God's people. The more someone means to God and His man, the more determined the evil one is to devour him.

How many times have we seen people, who were ready to take the next step with the LORD in His plan, fall to the adversary?

Bezaleel was a good man. The devil wants good men to turn back on God. If you are a good man, then know *"...Satan hath desired to have you..." **(Luke 22:31)**.* The Bible warns in **Matthew 24:43,** *"But know this, that if the goodman of the house had known in what watch the thief would come, he would have watched, and would not have suffered his house to be broken up."* The more we mean to God and His plan, the more intense the battle with evil will be in our life.

How does Satan attack the child of God? In this case, how did Satan attack Bezaleel? While Bezaleel was waiting for direction, this rebellion took place. He had to get past this uprising against Moses before he would see his part in God's plan for the ages. Did he have what it takes to move beyond this trouble in the camp?

Many fail to understand that there will be a testing between being equipped to serve the LORD and finding their place of service. Church history is filled with believers who fell to this trap set by the devil. The most difficult time in a child of God's life is when he is waiting on the LORD to see what's next for him.

Because of the seriousness of this lesson, I have divided it into three parts. These are three areas in which Bezaleel must not fail. These three areas are the same for us today.

Bezaleel and the Adversary
Part I: Will Bezaleel Join The Critical Crowd?

"And when the people saw that Moses delayed to come down out of the mount, the people gathered themselves together unto Aaron, and said unto him, Up, make us gods, which shall go before us; for as for this Moses, the man that brought us up out of the land of Egypt, we wot not what is become of him." **Exodus 32:1-6, v .1**

The first area in which Bezaleel was tested was the area of criticism. Look how quickly the people became critical of Moses. *"...For as for this Moses...."* What a way to talk about God's man. You can feel the contempt in their voices. Moses was getting something from God for them, and they became critical of him.

They criticized Moses because they did not understand his relationship with God. Moses was God's man, and Satan was behind this criticism of him and his leadership. If Bezaleel joined, then he would be finished. Notice what the Bible says in *I Samuel 26:9, "...Who can stretch forth his hand against the LORD'S anointed, and be guiltless?"*

It is a very dangerous thing to touch God's man or his leadership with our tongue *(I Timothy 5:19).* Never give ear to the criticism of leadership. Be careful about surrounding yourself with critical people.

1. Criticism Always Weakens Leadership And The Ability To Help People In The Time Of Need

Exodus 32:11, "And Moses besought the LORD his God, and said, LORD, why doth Thy wrath wax hot against Thy people, which Thou hast brought forth out of the land of Egypt with great power, and with a mighty hand?"

Moses was the only one who could help them, and they destroyed his influence with their tongue.

Often when young people are attacked by the evil one and his forces, the only people who could help them have been destroyed by criticism.

2. The LORD Does Not Use Critical People

Our words reflect our heart. If our heart is not right with God and others, our words will reveal it.

Psalm 19:14, *"Let the words of my mouth, and the meditation of my heart, be acceptable in Thy sight, O LORD, my strength, and my redeemer."*

The Word of God teaches us that our tongue is the hardest member of our body to keep under control.

James 3:4-10, v. 8, *"But the tongue can no man tame; it is an unruly evil, full of deadly poison."*

You will not find in the Word of God, or in church history, God using anyone who became critical of leadership. Being critical and negative about others will destroy your influence.

Nothing will destroy a person's future faster than the tongue. (Read again ***James 3:6-8***). Our tongue can start a fire that will burn up every good thing around us.

If Bezaleel joins in on the criticism of Moses, he is finished. The good news is that Bezaleel did not join in on the criticism of God's man. The question is then, will we keep a right heart and spirit toward leadership and the ones who have helped us become what we are?

LEARN THE POWER OF WORDS

Here are four truths that all believers should know about their words.

1. Our Words Reflect Our Heart

Matthew 12:35-36, *"A good man out of the good treasure of the heart bringeth forth good things: and an evil man out of the evil treasure bringeth forth evil things. But I say unto you, That every idle word that men shall speak, they shall give account thereof in the day of judgment."*

If we want to change our words, we must let the LORD change our heart. *Psalm 51:10,* *"Create in me a clean heart, O God; and renew a right spirit within me."*

2. Our Words Have Power

Proverbs 18:21, *"Death and life are in the power of the tongue: and they that love it shall eat the fruit thereof."*

Our words have the power of death or life. The more influence someone has, the more powerful their words are.

3. People With Wisdom Are Careful With Their Words

Proverbs 17:27-28, *"He that hath knowledge spareth his words: and a man of understanding is of an excellent spirit. Even a fool, when he holdeth his peace, is counted wise: and he that shutteth his lips is esteemed a man of understanding."*

Our wisdom and maturity in the LORD is measured in part by our words.

I Corinthians 13:11, *"When I was a child, I spake as a child, I understood as a child, I thought as a child: but when I became a man, I put away childish things."*

4. It Is The Duty Of All Believers To Encourage Someone Every Day

Hebrews 3:13, *"But exhort one another daily, while it is called To day; lest any of you be hardened through the deceitfulness of sin."*

If our goal is to encourage someone every day, we will not be a discouraging person. Make this one of your "daily duties." Start today!

4. It Is The Duty Of All Believers To Encourage Someone Every Day

BEZALEEL AND THE ADVERSARY
PART II: WILL BEZALEEL COMPROMISE HIS CONVICTIONS?

"And they rose up early on the morrow, and offered burnt offerings, and brought peace offerings; and the people sat down to eat and to drink, and rose up to play." **EXODUS 32:6-8, v. 6**

The second area in which Bezaleel was tested was is in his personal convictions. Moses was out of sight, and many were joining in on this little god worship. The LORD told Moses that the people *"...have corrupted themselves" (v. 7)*. Would Bezaleel corrupt himself? Would he join in and *"...eat...drink...and...play?"* No, he did not join in on their rebellion.

We live in a changing world, and many churches and Christians are changing with the world. We have many "Lot-minded believers" living in a "Gomorrah-minded world."

It takes a while for people to develop their personal convictions. People who compromise their personal convictions lose the life they could have had.

1. Our Personal Convictions Should Be Based On The Bible

God's Word will not change. *Psalm 119:89* says, *"For ever, O LORD, Thy word is settled in heaven."*

The things we believe should be the same things the first century believers received. We should commit to every generation *"...the same..." (II Timothy 2:2)*. If we change one thing, it is not the same. It has been said, "Things that are different are not the same."

2. Personal Convictions Help Us Stay Right And On Track

Psalm 31:3, *"For Thou art my rock and my fortress; therefore for Thy name's sake lead me, and guide me."*

Psalm 73:24, *"Thou shalt guide me with Thy counsel, and afterward receive me to glory."*

Two of the most difficult things to do in the Christian life are to stay right with God and to stay on track with our life. Personal convictions that are based on God's Word help us accomplish these two things.

Good news…Bezaleel did not compromise his personal convictions.

DEVELOPING PERSONAL CONVICTIONS

Here are four questions that help us to know what is right and help us to stay on track.

1. Is It Pleasing To The LORD?

John 8:29, *"And He that sent Me is with Me: the Father hath not left Me alone; for I do always those things that please Him."*

The LORD Jesus said, *"…I do always those things that please Him."* The highest goal of the Christian life is to please the LORD. If it will not please the LORD, don't do it!

2. Will It Hinder My Walk And Witness For Christ?

Hebrews 12:1-2, v. 1, *"Wherefore seeing we also are compassed about with so great a cloud of witnesses, let us lay aside every weight, and the sin which doth so easily beset us, and let us run with patience the race that is set before us"*

We do not want to pick up weight or sin. We are in a race. The LORD would never lead His children to pick up something that would hinder their race.

We want to be a faithful witness. The LORD would not lead His children to pick up something that would limit our witness.

If it will slow us down or limit our witness, say "No!"

3. Can I Thank God For It And Put My Heart In It?

Colossians 3:17, *"And whatsoever ye do in word or deed, do all in the name of the Lord Jesus, giving thanks to God and the Father by Him."*

Colossians 3:23, *"And whatsoever ye do, do it heartily, as to the Lord, and not unto men"*

Enthusiasm and excitement are the "spark" in the work of the LORD. People will follow excited people. We will not have excitement or joy if we cannot thank God for it and put our whole heart into it. If you cannot thank God for it and put your heart into it, don't do it!

4. Is There Doubt Concerning It?

Romans 14:23, *"And he that doubteth is damned if he eat, because he eateth not of faith: for whatsoever is not of faith is sin."*

There will always be that element of faith in unknowing, but doubt is a "red light." Wait until the LORD gives you the "green light." If your heart is right with God and you have strong doubt, wait!

When heeded, these four Bible truths will save you from a lot of heartache and disappointment.

Bezaleel and the Adversary
Part III: Will Bezaleel Use His Gift and Ability to Make the Golden Calf?

"...Up, make us gods...And all the people brake off the golden earrings which were in their ears, and brought them unto Aaron. And he received them at their hand, and fashioned it with a graving tool, after he had made it a molten calf: and they said, These be thy gods, O Israel, which brought thee up out of the land of Egypt." **Exodus 32:1-4**

The most gifted craftsman in all of Israel was Bezaleel. He had been taught by the masters in Egypt how to fashion works of gold. Yet, he did ***not*** make this golden calf.

In the book of Daniel, we read that Nebuchadnezzar, who is a type of the devil, wanted *"Children in whom was no blemish, but well favoured* (this describes Christians)... *whom they might teach the learning and the tongue of the Chaldeans" **(Daniel 1:4)**.*

The world wants the best, and the best is God's people. The world wants you. They want what you have been given from God for their lust. They want your gifts and abilities to be spent for them.

Sadly, we see and hear of those who grew up in church singing in the choir or working in the ministry "cashing in" for what the world will give them. The world and lust will one day pass away *(I John 2:15-17).*

How can we help believers say "No" to all that the world offers them? How can we help them use their gifts and abilities for the LORD and His work?

1. Understand That Our Gifts And Abilities Are From God

James 1:17, *"Every good gift and every perfect gift is from above, and cometh down from the Father of lights, with whom is no variableness, neither shadow of turning."*

We are not our own. There are no self-made men in the LORD's work. We are *"...His workmanship, created in Christ Jesus unto good works..." **(Ephesians 2:10).***

2. Believe That One Day We Will Give An Account Of Our Life To Him

II Corinthians 5:10, *"For we must all appear before the judgment seat of Christ; that every one may receive the things done in his body, according to that he hath done, whether it be good or bad."*

Our work will one day be tried by fire to see what sort it is.

I Corinthians 3:11-15, v. 14, *"If any man's work abide which he hath built thereupon, he shall receive a reward."*

The only life that really counts is the one given to the LORD ***(Mark 8:35).*** Every man should find a place of service in his local church ***(Matthew 28:19-20).***

Good news…Bezaleel did not "cash in" and "sell out" to the world to make their golden calf. The world is still making golden calves, and they want you.

USING YOUR GIFTS FOR GOD

"Every good gift and every perfect gift is from above, and cometh down from the Father of lights, with whom is no variableness, neither shadow of turning." **JAMES 1:17**

The LORD puts in His people all they need to accomplish His work. What has the LORD put in you?

1. Discover Your Gift

Ephesians 4:8, *"Wherefore He saith, When He ascended up on high, He led captivity captive, and gave gifts unto men."*

We will never understand all that God has given us until we give ourselves to the LORD. If you are a child of God, you have something to contribute. (Read again ***I Corinthians 12:12-26***.) What can you do?

2. Dedicate Yourself And Your Gift To God

Romans 12:1-2, v. 1, *"I beseech you therefore, brethren, by the mercies of God, that ye present your bodies a living sacrifice, holy, acceptable unto God, which is your reasonable service."*

We all must choose who we will serve ***(Joshua 24:15)***. The best decision any child of God can make is to give their life to the LORD. This is how we dedicate our gifts and abilities to the LORD.

3. Develop Your Gifts

Proverbs 27:17, *"Iron sharpeneth iron; so a man sharpeneth the countenance of his friend."*

We develop our gifts by getting around people who are "sharper" than we are. A great teacher can help a good teacher get better, a great singer can help a good singer get better, etc. Get around people who want you to be great.

4. Do Your Part

James 1:22, *"But be ye doers of the word, and not hearers only, deceiving your own selves."*

When it is all said and done, we must be doers - not just hearers. When I was a child, we had an expression, "There are too many chiefs and not enough Indians." Today we have too many chiefs and not enough believers. Be a doer!

Bezaleel had everything that he needed to accomplish God's will with his life. The will of God for Bezaleel was to help Moses do what God had called him to do. The LORD put in Bezaleel, while he was in Egypt, the skill, knowledge, and ability to build the Tabernacle.

God always puts His gifts for mankind in people. People are the real treasure in the LORD's work.

Satan wants all the treasures of the LORD. He has been successful down through the ages with his threefold attack. I have seen many gifted young men and women end their journey for God. In every case, it was in one of these three areas that they failed.

Paul said of our enemy, *"...For we are not ignorant of his devices" **(II Corinthians 2:11)**.* Bezaleel did not fall into the trap Satan set, and we do not have to fall into his trap either. Amen!

LESSON 9: BEZALEEL JOINS THE INNER CIRCLE

"And Moses said unto the children of Israel, See, the LORD hath called by name Bezaleel the son of Uri, the son of Hur, of the tribe of Judah"
EXODUS 35:30-35, v. 30

Bezaleel joined "Team Moses." Can you imagine being a part of the inner circle with Moses? To be on the inside and to see and hear what Bezaleel was privileged to see and hear would have been life changing. To work with this giant in the faith was an honour that few had.

The LORD Jesus had an inner circle. Peter, James, and John were inner circle disciples. These three men were on the mountain with Christ and heard the voice of God, they saw Moses and Elias, and they saw the LORD Jesus transfigured *(Matthew 17:1-6)*. These three disciples saw and heard many other things the rest of the disciples did not see and hear *(Mark 5:37, 13:3; Luke 8:51)*.

Paul had an inner circle. Churches have an inner circle. The inner circle of the church are the people who make the church "tick." They see what others do not see. They are the strength of the church. Every man should seek to be an inner circle Christian.

How did Bezaleel join the inner circle? What did he do while being part of the inner circle? How can every man become an inner circle Christian?

1. Moses Accepted Him

***Exodus 35:30**, "And Moses said unto the children of Israel, See, the LORD hath called by name Bezaleel..."*

We read in these verses where Moses was rehearsing with the children of Israel what the LORD had told him about Bezaleel. The LORD told Moses that He wanted Bezaleel to stand with him in the great work that He had given him to do.

Moses understood that Bezaleel was not a Joshua or a Caleb. He knew that the LORD had given this young man a special gift that was needed in the LORD's work. If Moses did not accept him, Bezaleel would not be able to do what God had called him to do.

The Golden Rule in the work of the LORD is to accept people for what they are and where they are. People are not all in the same place in their walk with the LORD, and they are not all on the same level in their Christian service.

Every church has four groups of people. There are leaders, workers, followers, and those to be reached.

- **Leaders**

  Leaders are those who have won personal victories, have surrendered their lives to do God's will, stand with leadership, have an understanding about the work of the LORD, maintain a good spirit, and want to help the pastor do what God has called him to do.

  These are the ones who accept the responsibility of the work of the LORD. Their lives challenge workers to do their best in the LORD's work.

- **Workers**

  Workers are those who have won personal victories, have surrendered their lives to do God's will, understand the work and ministry of the local church, have the right spirit, and are faithful to their place of service.

  These are the ones who want to help the pastor in the local church ministries. They love and accept followers and work with them to win personal victories. *(For more information on workers, read Lesson 7.)*

- **Followers**

  Followers are those who know Christ as their personal Saviour, have become members of the local church, and are winning personal victories.

  Followers have a desire to see their friends and loved ones come to Christ. They know more unsaved people than leaders or workers do and will reach them if helped.

  Our goal for a follower is for them to become a "Five Star Christian." This can be accomplished by doing five things consistently – reading your Bible daily, praying, being faithful to church, giving, and telling others about Christ.

- **Those to Be Reached**

  Those to be reached are the people who have not become members of the local church. They could be saved or unsaved.

  Those to be reached cannot help until they become a part of the local church. Our desire is to see everyone saved and part of the church.

To accept people where they are means that we understand the difference in leaders, workers, followers, and those to be reached; and we do not put them in a place of service where they will be hurt or hurt others.

2. Moses Allowed Him To Be What God Made Him

Exodus 35:31-33, v. 31*, "And he hath filled him with the spirit of God, in wisdom, in understanding, and in knowledge, and in all manner of workmanship"*

Bezaleel was a craftsman. He was not Caleb. Caleb could teach you how to fight and to take a city. Bezaleel could teach you how to make the sword.

In the book of Esther, there are four animals used to carry the messages *(post)* to the ends of the kingdom ***(Esther 8:10)****.* They used, *"...horseback...mules, camels, and young dromedaries."* Horses can go to nearby areas very quickly, mules can go up into mountains and down into valleys where horses cannot go, camels can carry heavy burdens great distances, but dromedaries can go great distances faster. The dromedary can <u>run</u> eighteen hours a day. It took all four to get the message to the people.

God gives us different kinds of people. It takes everyone working together to reach the world with the Gospel.

Moses let Bezaleel be Bezaleel.

3. Moses Allowed Him To Teach Others What He Knew

Exodus 35:34, *"And he hath put in his heart that he may teach, both he, and Aholiab, the son of Ahisamach, of the tribe of Dan."*

We will, in *Lesson 10,* talk about Bezaleel the teacher. What we need to understand in this lesson is that Moses allowed Bezaleel to teach others what he had been taught from the masters in Egypt. Bezaleel became part of Moses' trusted inner circle.

How Can I Be Part of the Inner Circle?

1. You Must Be The Right Kind Of Person

I Corinthians 8:3, "...If any man love God, the same is known of him."

Leaders want people close to them who know and love God and who have the right spirit. Leaders want to know, *"...Is thine heart right, as my heart is with thy heart? ...If it be...Come...see my zeal for the LORD" (II Kings 10:15-16).*

2. You Must Be The Kind Of Man God Speaks About Concerning Leadership

Acts 6:3, "Wherefore, brethren, look ye out among you seven men of honest report, full of the Holy Ghost and wisdom, whom we may appoint over this business."

This is not just part of the qualification for a deacon, this should be the goal of every man. God speaks to us in many other portions of the Scripture about the men we should put in leadership. Determine to be the kind of man that God speaks about to lead.

3. You Must Be Willing To Help God's Man

Matthew 28:19-20, "Go ye therefore, and teach all nations, baptizing them in the name of the Father, and of the Son, and of the Holy Ghost: Teaching them to observe all things whatsoever I have commanded you: and, lo, I am with you alway, even unto the end of the world. Amen."

The church is on a mission from God. Our mission is to take the Gospel to every person. The pastor of the church will one day give an account to the LORD for what the church has accomplished *(Hebrews 13:17).*

Notes

Many years ago, I made two life-changing decisions. First, I gave my life to do God's will. Second, I quit worrying about God's will *for* my life and started doing God's will *with* my life. The will of God for my life is to help others do the will of God with their life. I want to help people do the will of God with their life. If every believer would make these two life-changing decisions, they would have a good day at the Judgment Seat of Christ ***(II Corinthians 5:10)***.

LESSON 10: BEZALEEL, THE TEACHER

"And He hath put in his heart that he may teach, both he, and Aholiab, the son of Ahisamach, of the tribe of Dan." **EXODUS 35:30-35, v. 34**

The LORD called Moses to do something that was impossible for one man to do. He called him to build the Tabernacle. The building of the Tabernacle in the wilderness was going to require everyone's involvement.

Bezaleel was going to teach the children of Israel how to do what God had called them to do. He was their teacher. Bezaleel knew what to teach, and he had a heart to teach people.

The only way that truth goes from generation to generation is for someone to teach it. If we do not teach the next generation what we have been taught, it will be lost. Thank the LORD for the people who teach others how to do the work of the LORD.

Here are some questions to consider when thinking about teaching others.

1. Why Should We Teach Others?

Luke 1:50, *"And His mercy is on them that fear Him from generation to generation."*

Acts 13:36a, *"For David, after he had served his own generation by the will of God, fell on sleep…"*

Bezaleel was not the first believer in his family's history, but he could have been the last one.

The only way that truth goes from generation to generation is because someone is committed to teach it. You may be the first believer in your family, but you can start a godly heritage.

2. Who Are We To Teach?

II Timothy 2:2, *"And the things that thou hast heard of me among many witnesses, the same commit thou to faithful men, who shall be able to teach others also."*

We are to teach faithful men. Men who have proven themselves to be faithful are to be prepared by the generation that has gone on before them.

Every man is to pass on to the next generation what he has been given. Find a faithful man and invest your life in him.

3. What Are We To Teach?

Acts 2:42, *"And they continued stedfastly in the apostles' doctrine and fellowship, and in breaking of bread, and in prayers."*

Matthew 28:20, *"Teaching them to observe all things whatsoever I have commanded you: and, lo, I am with you alway, even unto the end of the world. Amen."*

We trace our spiritual heritage back to and are continuing in the apostles' doctrine. We are to teach the *"...same..."* that we have been taught ***(II Timothy 2:2)***. The body of doctrine that we have been given is the same body of doctrine we are to teach.

4. How Are We To Teach?

John 13:15, "For I have given you an example, that ye should do as I have done to you."

We are to teach by example. We are the only Bible that some people will read.

I Timothy 4:12, "Let no man despise thy youth; but be thou an example of the believers, in word, in conversation, in charity, in spirit, in faith, in purity."

- *In word* = Let the Word of God be the final authority.

- *In conversation* = Let the words of our mouth be pleasing to the Lord.

- *In charity* = Have a heart for people (compassion).

- *In spirit* = Keep a godly spirit about the things of the LORD.

- *In purity* = Live above reproach.

WHAT IS THE MOST IMPORTANT THING ABOUT TEACHING?

1. How We Teach is Important

Mark 4:2, "And He taught them many things by parables, and said unto them in His doctrine"

The LORD Jesus used many methods of teaching. He used stories (parables); He used children; He used birds, rocks, flowers, and trees; He *"...taught the people out of the ship..." (Luke 5:3)*. He was the Master teacher. He is our example.

Every teacher should want to improve his methods of teaching. *How* we teach is important.

2. What We Teach Is <u>More</u> Important

Matthew 7:28b-29, *"...The people were astonished at His doctrine: For He taught them as one having authority, and not as the scribes."*

The LORD Jesus knew that what people believe determines how they live. People need to be taught the Word of God and the doctrine that we have been given. Doctrine is our body of belief.

Paul said, *"...Thou hast fully known my doctrine, manner of life..." (**II Timothy 3:10).* What he believed *("...my doctrine...")*, determined how he lived *("...my manner of life...").*

What we teach is more important.

3. How We Live Is The <u>Most</u> Important

Acts 6:3, *"...Look ye out among you...men of honest report..."*

Acts 22:12, *"And one Ananias, a devout man according to the law, having a good report of all the Jews which dwelt there"*

I Timothy 3:7, *"Moreover he must have a good report of them which are without; lest he fall into reproach and the snare of the devil."*

These verses help us to see that men who are to serve the LORD must live right.

One of the highest compliments that can be paid to a man is, "He is a good man."

Acts 11:24, *"For he was a good man, and full of the Holy Ghost and of faith: and much people was added unto the Lord."*

Bezaleel was a good man, and he was a good teacher.

Lesson 11: Bezaleel, Finished and Approved

"And Bezaleel the son of Uri, the son of Hur, of the tribe of Judah, made all that the LORD commanded Moses." **Exodus 38:22**

"Thus was all the work of the tabernacle of the tent of the congregation finished: and the children of Israel did according to all that the LORD commanded Moses, so did they." **Exodus 39:32**

God told Moses that He would come down *(Exodus 3:8)* and deliver His people. Moses took the people out of Egypt to *"...meet with God..." (Exodus 19:17)*.

The purpose of the Tabernacle was to provide a place where the LORD could meet with people. He said, *"And there I will meet with the children of Israel, and the tabernacle shall be sanctified by My glory" (Exodus 29:43).*

(Every serious-minded believer should be familiar with the Tabernacle in the wilderness, a subject I love to speak on, but in these lessons have limited myself.)

The Tabernacle was finished. It was dedicated to the LORD, and the fire came down. The Tabernacle was finished and approved.

It is amazing that this *"...mixed multitude..."* that came out of Egypt accomplished such a powerful work for God. Who would have believed it?

I am sure that one day we will feel the same about what this generation of believers has accomplished.

1. Bezaleel Finished What God Gave Him To Do

Exodus 38:22, *"And Bezaleel the son of Uri, the son of Hur, of the tribe of Judah, made all that the LORD commanded Moses."*

We spend a lot of time celebrating when people start. The LORD wants us to have a good ending.

Ecclesiastes 7:8, *"Better is the end of a thing than the beginning thereof: and the patient in spirit is better than the proud in spirit."*

How are you going to finish?

2. The Children of Israel Finished The Work God Gave Them To Do

Exodus 39:32, *"Thus was all the work of the tabernacle of the tent of the congregation finished: and the children of Israel did according to all that the LORD commanded Moses, so did they."*

They had accomplished something with their life that all the generations to follow could enjoy.

Their life's work made it possible for generations to come to have a place to meet with God.

3. Moses Approved The Finished Work

Exodus 39:42-43, v. 43, *"And Moses did look upon all the work, and, behold, they had done it as the LORD had commanded, even so had they done it: and Moses blessed them."*

Moses saw on this earth what God had put in his heart and mind to do.

Great people are thankful people, and Moses knew how to say, "Thank You." The Bible says, *"...And Moses blessed them...."* Think about what that blessing meant to the children of Israel and to Bezaleel.

How Did This Mixed Multitude Do It?

1. They Followed God's Plan

Exodus 39:42, *"According to all that the LORD commanded Moses, so the children of Israel made all the work."*

The Tabernacle was built *"...according to..."* God's plan.

If we want to see the work of the LORD accomplished, we must work according to God's plan.

(Matthew 28:19-20, Mark 16:15, Acts 1:8)

2. They Followed Moses, God's Man

Exodus 39:43*, "And Moses did look upon all the work, and, behold, they had done it as the LORD had commanded, even so had they done it: and Moses blessed them."*

Moses was God's man, and the LORD had given him what people needed.

If a person is not a good follower, they will not be a good leader one day.

Paul said to the church at Thessalonica, *"And ye became followers of **us**, and of the Lord..."* ***I Thessalonians 1:6***

3. They Worked Together as a Team

Exodus 39:32, *"...And the children of Israel did..."*

God does not call each one by name. He just says, *"...The children of Israel made all the work"* ***(Exodus 39:42).***

Big shots are not team players. It has been said over and over, but it is true. TEAM spells: **T**ogether **E**veryone **A**ccomplishes **M**ore.

Be a team player.

4. They Used the Resources God Gave Them

Exodus 36:5, *"And they spake unto Moses, saying, The people bring much more than enough for the service of the work, which the LORD commanded to make."*

The people gave so much that Moses had to tell them to quit giving ***(Exodus 36:6).*** Amazing, that is not the case today. Today we have a generation of believers who try to make all they can and can all they make.

Nothing great for God will ever be accomplished without making a real sacrifice.

Remember it is never money that we need. The great need in the work of the LORD is people. *"...The labourers are few...."* We need people who will give what the LORD has put in their hands.

The people used three things that God had given them.

- **They used the <u>Treasure</u> they brought from Egypt.**

  Exodus 3:22, *"But every woman shall borrow of her neighbour, and of her that sojourneth in her house, jewels of silver, and jewels of gold, and raiment: and ye shall put them upon your sons, and upon your daughters; and ye shall spoil the Egyptians."*

  Exodus 36:3, *"And they received of Moses all the offering, which the children of Israel had brought for the work of the service of the sanctuary, to make it withal. And they brought yet unto him free offerings every morning."*

  Exodus 36:7, *"For the stuff they had was sufficient for all the work to make it, and too much."*

  They did not hold back. God always puts in His children's hands everything needed for His work. We are stewards of God's wealth.

- **They used the <u>Time</u> God gave them.**

  Exodus 36:3, *"...every morning."*

  Every day, there was something to do. Time is our personal treasure. It takes time to build something for the LORD.

- **They used their God-given <u>Talent.</u>**

  Exodus 36:4, *"And all the wise men, that wrought all the work of the sanctuary, came every man from his work which they made"*

  Everyone did what they could. They did that in which they were gifted.

  Our gifts and abilities are given to us for two reasons - to provide for our families and to provide for the LORD's work.

Be a good steward of all three.

LESSON 12: HOW TO BE A BEZALEEL

B - Be a Believer

Exodus 31:3a, *"...I have filled him with the spirit of God..."*

You must first be a believer. Only believers are filled with the Holy Spirit.

Are you a believer?

Acts 5:14, *"And believers were the more added to the Lord, multitudes both of men and women"*

E – Empty Self

Exodus 31:3a, *"...I have filled him..."*

God cannot fill what is already full. We must empty ourselves of the things that take the place of the LORD.

I John 2:15-17, *"Love not the world, neither the things that are in the world. If any man love the world, the love of the Father is not in him. For all that is in the world, the lust of the flesh, and the lust of the eyes, and the pride of life, is not of the Father, but is of the world. And the world passeth away, and the lust thereof: but he that doeth the will of God abideth for ever."*

𝒵 – Zeal for God's Work

Exodus 38:22, *"And Bezaleel ... made all that the LORD commanded Moses."*

Desire and zeal are the things that fuel the Christian life. Nothing has ever been accomplished for God without zeal and desire for the work of the LORD *(John 2:17, II Corinthians 9:2).*

Psalm 69:9*, "For the zeal of Thine house hath eaten me up; and the reproaches of them that reproached Thee are fallen upon me."*

𝒜 – Advance the Cause of Christ

Philippians 1:12, *"But I would ye should understand, brethren, that the things which happened unto me have fallen out rather unto the furtherance of the gospel"*

When it is all said and done, will people say about our life that we advanced the cause of Christ?

ℒ – Love People and See their Worth

John 13:35, *"By this shall all men know that ye are My disciples, if ye have love one to another."*

It is true that people do not care how much you know until they know how much you care.

Men who make a difference are men who love people and see their worth.

E – **Equip Others to Serve**

Ephesians 4:11-12, v. 12, *"For the perfecting of the saints, for the work of the ministry, for the edifying of the body of Christ"*

Take the time to train and help people. Invest your life in the next generation.

We all have been touched by others. We have their labour in us.

E – **Encourage Someone Every Day**

Hebrews 3:13, *"But exhort one another daily, while it is called To day; lest any of you be hardened through the deceitfulness of sin."*

Most people need a pat on the back and to hear "That a boy" to keep going for the LORD.

Our encouragement could make the difference in someone going forward for the LORD or turning back on the LORD.

L – **Look Up**

Hebrews 12:1-2, v. 2, *"Looking unto Jesus the author and finisher of our faith; who for the joy that was set before Him endured the cross, despising the shame, and is set down at the right hand of the throne of God."*

We are looking for our coming King. This generation of believers is closer to the coming of Christ than any other generation that has ever lived.

Keep looking up!

GOD LOVES YOU

*"For God so loved the world, that He gave His only begotten Son,
that whosoever believeth in Him should not perish,
but have everlasting life"* ***(John 3:16)***.

This great Bible verse reveals four truths from the heart of God for all people.

We are Loved

God wants us to know that **we are loved**. The Lord Jesus said, *"For God so loved the world...."*

You are a part of this world, and God loves you. He gave His Son for you, and He wants you *"...to know the love of Christ..."* ***(Ephesians 3:19)***.

We are of Worth

The Lord also wants us to know that **we are of worth**. We are so dear to God *"...that He gave His only begotten Son...."*

The Bible teaches us that we are all sinners. *"For all have sinned, and come short of the glory of God"* ***(Romans 3:23)***.

And sin must be paid for. *"For the wages of sin is death..."* ***(Romans 6:23)***.

But the Bible also teaches us that *"...Christ died for our sins according to the scriptures"* ***(I Corinthians 15:3)***.

God demonstrated His love for us and our worth to Him when He sent His Son to die in our place.

The good news is that the Lord Jesus paid our sin debt in full when He died on the cross. *"For He hath made Him to be sin for us..."* **(II Corinthians 5:21)**.

Christ loved us and gave Himself for us as payment for our sin.

You may ask, "How can God forgive **my** sin?" He can because of what Jesus did.   *"...While we were yet sinners, Christ died for us"* **(Romans 5:8)**.

We can have Hope

God wants us to know that **we can have hope**. He said *"...that whosoever believeth in Him should not perish...."*

Life is fragile, and people are perishing. But Christ came *"...that they might have life, and that they might have it more abundantly"* **(John 10:10)**.

In a world where so many have lost hope, God wants us to know that the *"...Lord Jesus Christ...is our hope"* **(I Timothy 1:1)**.

He rose from the dead, and He said, *"...Because I live, ye shall live also"* **(John 14:19)**.

We can have Purpose

God wants us to know that **we can have purpose** in life. He desires that we *"...should not perish, but have everlasting life."*

"And this is the promise that He hath promised us, even eternal life" **(I John 2:25)**.

You may ask, "How can **I** receive God's promise of eternal life?"

Acknowledge that you are a sinner, *"For all have sinned, and come short of the glory of God" **(Romans 3:23)***.

Believe that the Lord Jesus died for you, for *"Christ died for our sins according to the scriptures" **(I Corinthians 15:3)***.

Call upon the Lord to save you, *"For whosoever shall call upon the name of the Lord shall be saved" **(Romans 10:13)***.

If you would be willing to turn to Christ in repentance and faith, pray this simple prayer of salvation:

> *LORD, I know that I am a sinner, and I believe You*
> *died and rose again for me. I am trusting You to*
> *forgive me, come into my heart and save me. Help me*
> *to live for You. In Jesus' name, Amen.*

The Lord Jesus said, *"...I give unto them eternal life; and they shall never perish..." **(John 10:28)***.

Everlasting life is ours when we receive Christ as our personal Saviour.

NOW THAT YOU ARE A CHRISTIAN:

- Share your new-found faith with your family and friends *(Acts 16:31-33)*.

- Identify with Christ through believer's baptism and become part of a local, Bible-believing church *(Acts 2:41, 47)*.